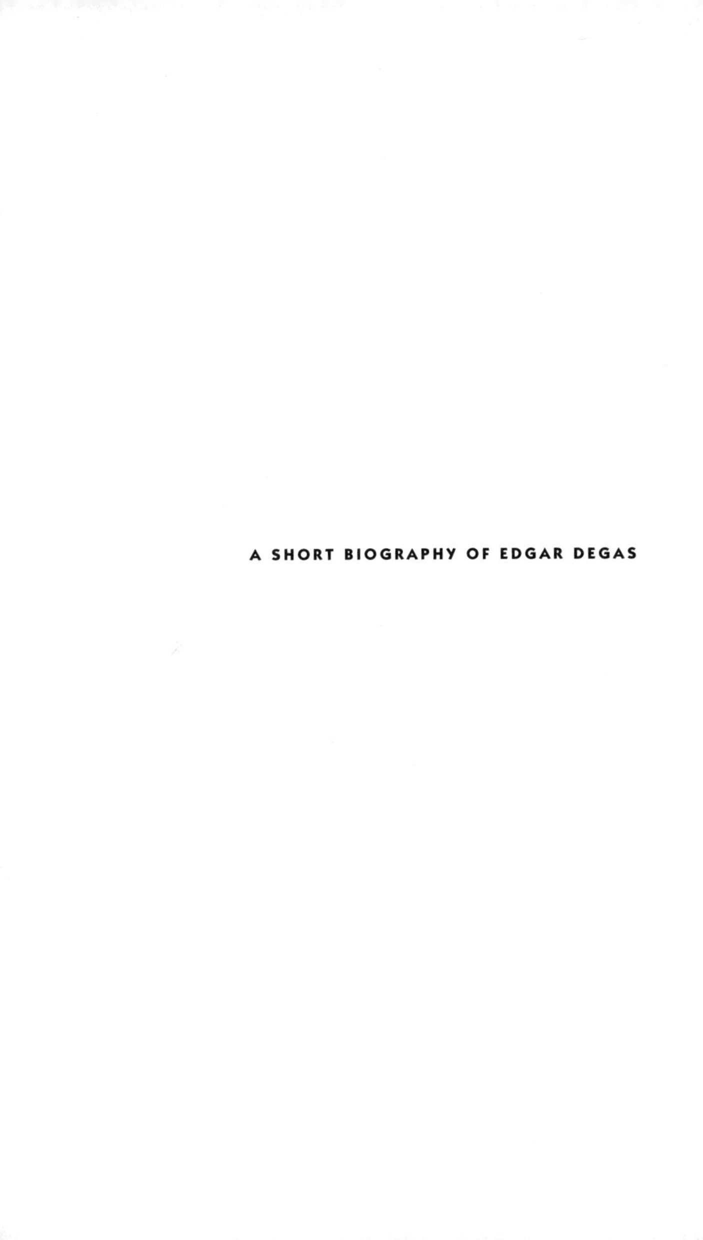

A SHORT BIOGRAPHY OF EDGAR DEGAS

A SHORT BIOGRAPHY OF
Edgar Degas

Susan DeLand

B BENNA BOOKS

A Boutique Press for Artists & Writers

Carlisle, Massachusetts

A Short Biography of Edgar Degas

Series Editor: Susan DeLand
Written by: Susan DeLand

To Allan McLean DeLand

978-1-944038-14-4

Front Cover: Edgar Degas (French, 1834–1917), *Self-Portrait*, 1857–1858
oil on paper, laid down on canvas
The J. Paul Getty Museum, Los Angeles
Digital image courtesy of the Getty's Open Content Program
Back Cover: Hilaire-Germain-Edgar Degas
The Rehearsal, c. 1873–1878
Oil on canvas; 47.2 x 61.5 cm (18 9/16 x 24 3/16 in.)
Framed: 71.9 x 87.2 x 11.2 cm (28 5/16 x 34 5/16 x 4 7/16 in.)
Harvard Art Museums/Fogg Museum, Bequest from the Collection of
Maurice Wertheim, Class of 1906, 1951.47
Photo: Imaging Department © President and Fellows of Harvard College

Published by Benna Books
an imprint of Applewood Books
Carlisle, Massachusetts 01741

To request a free copy of our current catalog
featuring our best-selling books, write to:
Applewood Books
P.O. Box 27
Carlisle, MA 01741
Or visit us on the web at: www.awb.com

10 9 8 7 6 5 4 3 2 1
MANUFACTURED IN THE UNITED STATES OF AMERICA

HILAIRE-GERMAIN-EDGAR DE GAS was born in Paris, France, on July 19, 1834. Better known to the world as Edgar Degas, his names were given to honor his grandfathers: Germain Musson and René-Hilaire Degas. Edgar was the eldest of five children: Achille, born in Paris in 1838; Thérese, born in Naples, Italy, in 1840; followed by Marguerite in 1842; and the youngest, René, born in Paris in 1845.

Edgar's father, L. P. Auguste-Hyacinthe Degas was born in Naples, Italy, in 1807.

Auguste's father, René-Hilaire, had fled the French Revolution and started a banking firm called Degas Padre e Figli in Naples. Edgar's grandfather made a fortune as a money changer in the Napoleonic wars. He had a luxury home in Paris and a palazzo in Naples. Following the family business, as an adult, Auguste opened a branch of the bank in Paris, where he provided a comfortable life for his family enriched with music, theater, and art. He frequently held musical recitals in the de Gas home. The family name was traditionally spelled *Degas*, but Auguste harbored some pretensions that led him to change the spelling to *de Gas*. This slight adjustment implied aristocratic land ownership and nobility. Auguste went as far as applying for a patent of nobility, similar to a coat of arms, as "La Famille de Gas." This was an odd decision in light of his own father's flight from France. Edgar did not share his father's frivolous aspirations and reverted to the original spelling of Degas in his late thirties. He was the only family member to do so.

Marie-Celéstine Musson, Edgar's American mother, was born in New Orleans, Louisiana, in 1815 of a prominent Creole family. Her mother descended from the original French and Spanish settlers of New Orleans. Marie-Celéstine's father, Germain, had fled his native Haiti after the revolution led by Toussaint Louverture and settled in New Orleans. Germain made a fortune in cotton and Mexican silver and had both a plantation on the Mississippi Delta and a sumptuous mansion on the Vieux Carré. Celéstine was the youngest daughter of Germain Musson and Marie-Céleste Rilleux. Her mother died at the age of twenty-five. Germain, saddened by the death of his wife, took Celéstine and her older brother Michel to France to be educated.

Celéstine, an amateur opera singer, fell in love with her Parisian neighbor, Auguste, and they married in 1832, when she was eighteen. To celebrate the birth of her first child, and likely to create an American link, her father purchased a Creole cottage in New Orleans on North Rampart Street in little Edgar's name. Many years later, Degas would make an extended visit to New Orleans that would have a lasting effect on his art.

Edgar had a fluid childhood, living in both France and Italy. Degas exhibited notable skill for drawing and painting from a young age. In 1845, when he was eleven years old, he was enrolled in Lycée Louis-le-Grand, a prestigious and rigorous all-boy's secondary school in the 5th arrondissement of Paris, known as the Latin Quarter. Latin was the language of education dating from the founding of the Sorbonne in 1257.

Here he befriended Ludovic Halévy and Paul Valpinçon, who would remain close friends for most of their lives. Edgar received a classical education, learning the language and literature of the ancient world and classical French.

In 1847, when Edgar was thirteen, his mother died. Her loss had a profound effect on Degas, who would later depict mother figures who were ill, sad, and mournful. When he graduated in 1853, Auguste expected Edgar to go into the family business of banking. Showing no interest, when he was nineteen, Degas went to Université de Paris to study law. The same year, he was accepted at the Musée du Louvre as a copyist. This was common practice in nineteenth-century Europe, and the primary way that aspiring artists developed technique was by imitating the masters. Edgar made notable copies of works by Raphael as well as contemporary painters Eugène Delacroix, a leader of the French Romantic school of art, and Jean-Auguste-Dominique Ingres, a French neoclassical painter. Through this focused training and the time spent at the Louvre, he developed an intense drawing style that had its roots in classical linear depictions.

In 1855, Degas enrolled in the École

The law was not to be Degas's future. After one year at Université, he left.

des Beaux-Arts in Paris. Founded in 1671, it was the most distinguished art school in France. Degas studied there for a year and then left to spend the next three years traveling and painting in Italy. His father was highly knowledgeable about early Italian art, and Edgar had grown up accompanying him to galleries and meeting with collectors. His father introduced him to Ingres, who told Edgar to "draw lines, lots of lines, either from memory or from nature."

Degas painted a beautiful portrait of his youngest brother, René. This may have been what convinced his father to back Degas's independent foray into self-education. Beginning in 1856, he traveled to Naples, Rome, and Florence. He sketched and painted in the Uffizi Gallery and in the Vatican. He made meticulous copies of Michelangelo and da Vinci and other Old Masters. During his time in Italy, Edgar practiced portraiture on himself. He made more than fifteen self-portraits in three years.

In 1858, Degas painted a masterful portrait of the Bellelli family, titled *The Family*. It featured his aunt Laure Bellelli and her husband, the baron Gennaro Bellelli, with their daughters, Giulia and Giovanna. It is an emotional family portrait. The baron, a political journalist, was banished from his home city, Naples, because of his actions in the revolution of 1848 that attempted to free Italian states from Austrian rule. At the time of the painting, the family was living in exile in Florence. Aunt Laure is pregnant and mourning her recently deceased father, Hilaire, whose portrait Degas hangs on a wall behind the family scene. The two daughters radiate tension, one enveloped by the mother and the other reaching for her distant father, positioned with his back to the viewer. This is considered Degas's first masterpiece and is the precursor of many of his paintings and sketches that give the sense that the viewer has caught a private moment, waiting a beat, as if to see what will transpire next.

Edgar drew constantly, took notes, and jotted down ideas and observations in his many illustrated notebooks. In one he wrote, "I must thoroughly realize I know nothing at all; it is the only way to get ahead." Thirty-eight of Degas's notebooks exist today, and they are a window into his journey. The earliest is dated in the mid-1850s, and they go through the 1880s. The pages contain caricatures of friends, studies for paintings, and composition sketches. They also have scribbled notes, appointments, addresses, names, titles of opera and theater performances he attended, travelogues, literary references, and insertions by his friends and teachers.

"Drawing is the artist's most direct and spontaneous expression, a species of writing: it reveals, better than does painting, his true personality."

Edgar returned to Paris and began to

put ordinary people and scenes into a modern context. Horse racing was popular among the Parisian bourgeoisie, and the racetracks were a fashionable place to be seen. Degas and his friends frequented the tracks, and he captured movement and form on his canvas. He also began to paint the invisible subjects: the laundresses, milliners, cleaners, and other women at work. He was developing composition with focal points outside of the traditional. In one race scene, the action of a nervous thoroughbred at the gate is all but ignored; the focus is on the last few horses in the lineup. Degas also portrayed milliners in a shop decorating hats. Their faces can barely be seen, but their working hands and scraps of colorful ribbon are at the forefront of the painting.

Soon paintings began to emerge that also reflected his social life. Degas had a love of opera, theater, and the ballet. The notebooks are filled with extraordinary drawings and studies depicting dancers, nudes, and fabric draping for costumes. In 1862, Degas met fellow painter Édouard Manet at the Louvre. Like other artists of the period, Degas and Manet shared both common ideals and competition. Degas grew to share Manet's disdain for the art establishment and the belief in more modern techniques and subject matter.

In 1868, Degas became a member of a group of renegade artists that included Claude Monet, Pierre-Auguste Renoir, Manet, and Alfred Sisley. This passionate group gathered at the Café Guerbois to speculate and discuss how artists would engage in the contemporary world. These meetings lined up with tumultuous times in France's history.

In 1870, France declared war on Germany, even though they were unprepared for modern warfare and suffered. Degas joined the national guard, and it is thought that he injured his eye while defending Paris. Paris was taken by the Germans, and then, with the collapse of

Napoleon III's Second Empire, the city was recaptured by the Paris Commune. France's defeat by the Germans led to *revanchism* (literally, revengeism), a deep and bitter hatred for Germany. Civil conflict quickly ensued between the Paris Commune and the French national government. Before long, with much bloodshed during *La Semaine Sanglante,* the communards were crushed by the national government. The prewar traditional France was conquered externally and internally. From this, an artistic revolution found its footing.

In 1870, Degas's brothers René and Achille had moved to New Orleans to start a business in the cotton trade, rejecting their father's expectation to carry on the family banking business. René had married, and his wife was expecting a child. The brothers continued their father's affectation, spelling their name de Gas and flourishing the faux coat of arms. Somehow, this worked in fading New Orleans, where there was no willingness to embrace the post–Civil War American culture that diminished the Creoles' social status. The Mussons continued to speak French and attempted to preserve the illusion of the *Ancien Régime* life: a box at the opera, the mansion on Esplanade Avenue. This was a sad façade. The opera closed, and the mansion was rented. Their great wealth was dwindling with their lifestyle.

Though the Mussons were out of step with the changing times, New Orleans itself was blooming. It was becoming an important city, rivaling the port of New York. Degas, thirty-eight years old and exhausted from the war and chaos of Paris, accepted an invitation to get to know his maternal relatives. He arrived in this city in transition and immersed himself in painting his family and the life so different from Paris and the bloodshed of war. He was there less than six months between the New Orleans holidays of All Saint's Day and Mardi Gras. While in New Orleans, he painted *Le*

Bureau de coton à La Nouvelle-Orléans (The Cotton Office in New Orleans) in 1873. Here he captured the lethargy of a slow day of commerce. He brought this painting back to Paris, and it became the first painting he sold to a museum, the Musée des Beaux-Arts de Pau in the Pyrenees.

Edgar returned to Paris in 1873, and not long after, his father died. For several years, family problems would consume Degas. The family bank failed, and Degas discovered that his brother René had catastrophic business debts and had lost much of the family money. René was trouble. He had fled from Paris to New Orleans because of a scandalous duel with his mistress's husband and his debts. There he married his cousin and then divorced her. To avoid bankruptcy and preserve the family name and reputation, Edgar sold his house and art collection to cover René's debt.

Upon his return to Paris, Degas witnessed the reconstruction of the city the

Degas disdainfully noted at the time that he would be forced to make a living off his art.

war had destroyed. Surveying the works of painters in Paris as it rebuilt buildings and neighborhoods, we have a record of the new colorful grand avenues, the reopened theaters, and the mingling of Parisians on the streets, in the shops, attending the ballet and the opera. Degas painted people where social classes intersected: on the streets and in the public gardens. He focused on capturing the people of the city in their occupations: singers, ballet dancers, and working men. Degas visited the rehearsal rooms and backstage of the ballet. He filled his notebooks with sketches of dancers tying their pointe shoes, adjusting their ethereal costumes, practicing at the barre, stretching, and performing. Degas created movement and drama by manipulating the viewer's relationship to the subject. At times, the ballerinas are seen from above, as if sitting in the balcony. At other times, the dance is seen from the orchestra pit or the side of the stage. A sketch of an opera singer in full aria places the viewer just behind, looking over her shoulder. These meticulous yet lively sketches would inform rich and nuanced images worked in oils or pastels in Edgar's studio. Degas was relentless in his exploration of color and shape. He studied and painted texture and movement in different contexts to understand it. If he wanted to paint smoke, his notes leave us a record of lists: smokers' pipes, cigarettes, cigars, locomotives, factory chimneys, steamboats. For painting bread: large, oval, long, round, shades of flour colors.

It was during this time period that Degas joined forces with Claude Monet, Alfred Sisley, Paul Gauguin, Édouard Manet, Pierre-Auguste Renoir, and other painters to challenge the old-school protocol for exhibiting their work. They rebelled against the juried system that forced their experimental work to be judged against the long-accepted techniques of realism. Their *Société anonyme des artistes* mounted exhibitions

of their own and others' work independent of the judgment of the Salon of
the Académie des Beaux-Arts. The role
of the Académie, founded in 1803, was
to protect and develop France's artistic
heritage. Its elite members were elected
for life and for their traditional values.
Many of them were the jurors for art-
works included in the Salon exhibitions.
These jurors abhorred the freestyle techniques of the Impressionists and barred
them from exhibiting.

*"Only when he no longer knows
what he is doing does the painter
do good things."*

**Though he was
a founding
member,
Edgar did not
identify with
the *plein air*
impressionists;
he considered
himself a
realist.**

Degas participated in six exhibitions
mounted by the Société between 1874
and 1886. His subjects were drawn from
urban life, and his careful drawings came
from analyzing every gesture and pose
of his subject. His methods and process
were far removed from the spontaneity
of his fellow artists. Degas experimented

with several media: painting, drawing, pastels, sculpture, and photography.

Sculpting used a different set of Edgar's skills. Unlike his hand controlling a brush, his fingers explored the soft clay and taught his hands the anatomy of a figure. He was not creating sculpture as art, to stand alone. He did not have them cast in bronze. He combined unusual materials, such as dressing his young ballerina, made of pigmented beeswax and found materials, in a five-tiered tulle skirt, fabric bodice and shoes, and a horsehair wig tied with a ribbon: *Little Dancer Aged Fourteen*. He considered the sculptures studies of movement and placement for his pastels and paintings—much like sketches. He worked in wax, clay, and malleable plastiline. Degas exhibited *Little Dancer* under a glass dome. It received mixed reviews, some complimenting the modernity of the subject and others outraged at his realist depiction. *Little Dancer* was not cast in bronze until

This sculpture was the only one Degas exhibited in his lifetime, although close to 150 were discovered in his studio after his death.

after Degas's death. The fabric ribbon around the metal hair and fabric tutu were the decisions of his heirs. In fact, the wax sculpture was badly deteriorated and had to be reconstructed to make the casting mold.

Today's image of a ballerina is one of intense discipline, professionalism, and physical prowess embodied in graceful poses. The ballet of Degas's day was scrappy. The model, young Marie Geneviève van Goethem, was the daughter of a laundress and, with her sisters, likely joined the ballet as a way out of poverty. She was fourteen years old when Degas sculpted her. She may have danced by day and been a prostitute by night. Her posture and expression are not those of an elegant prima ballerina. She is depicted as almost removed, sullen, disconnected from the cultural richness of the opera ballet. Marie dropped out of the ballet not long after Degas sculpted her and disappeared. Her sister Antoinette was jailed for theft, but another sister, known as Charlotte, devoted her life to the ballet, performing and then teaching at the Paris Opera Ballet for fifty-three years.

Edgar Degas had become a strong personality in his group: he was irascible and cynical, with a cutting sense of humor. He appeared disengaged romantically, having interactions with prostitutes but never having a loving and lasting relationship. Degas never married. Some have conjectured that his close friendship with painter Mary Cassatt was his great love, but his capacity for this is in question. He seemed to be incapable of intimacy or emotional commitment with women. He studied and sketched the female form as nudes, bathers, and ballet dancers. He made wax and clay sculptures, many of female bodies, kneading and shaping them to fully evoke the fluidity of their form. It is reported that he spent hours brushing a model's hair before sketching. His hands held intimate knowledge, but his heart did not.

Even before Degas met Cassatt, he saw one of her paintings and said, "There is someone who feels as I do." This from a man who said he didn't have much affection and wanted to "finish his life and die alone, with no happiness whatever." Likewise, Mary saw a pastel by Degas through a gallery window and said that she was dazzled by it. They met in Paris and began exhibiting and working closely. Ten years his junior, Cassatt began as the pupil, but soon drew her own share of attention. She introduced the use of metallic paint to create light and texture, and Edgar embraced it in his own art. Edgar painted within her paintings, giving them unusual perspective to increase depth. Degas sketched and painted Cassatt many times, often from the back, using the angular line of her posture to evoke emotions. One portrait of

Cassatt has her sitting, leaning in, a fan of *cartes de visite* in her hands. Artists often used these small cards to document their work. By including this small detail, Degas draws attention to her success as an artist. She was the only American to exhibit with the Impressionists, though she adhered to Degas's stand that she was not an Impressionist. Mary's friend Louisine Havemeyer, an early collector of Degas's work, commented on the difficulty of getting along with the cantankerous artist. Cassatt responded, "Oh, I am independent! I can live alone and I love to work," and said he disliked that "he couldn't find a chink in my armor."

Degas's longtime friendship with the novelist and librettist Ludovic Halévy and his wife, Louise, was a large part of his social life. Ludovic wrote romance novels and notably the libretto for Bizet's *Carmen*. The Halévy home was a lively salon for the disruptive artists, writers, musicians, and intellectuals of Paris. The guest list read: Marcel Proust, Guy de Maupassant, Alexandre Dumas, Henry James, and many of the Impressionist painters, and Degas was an incessant sketcher of the motley group. Degas's notebooks record the stories of friends observed: lively gestures, flowing wine, amorous intrigues, heated arguments, and sly caricatures. On the scruffy linen cover of a notebook dated 1877 titled "Croquis de Degas" (Sketches by Degas), splashes of spilled wine and smudges of food show the evidence of use. The sketchbooks are also filled with studies for paintings or pastels. Edgar worked and reworked the sketches until he caught the movement perfectly.

By the late 1800s, Degas was a successful artist and a collector of art that impressed him. He owned many of Mary Cassatt's paintings as well as works by friends Camille Pissarro, Paul Cézanne, Paul Gauguin, and Édouard Manet. His collection also included artists he revered: El Greco, Jean-Auguste-Dominique Ingres, Eugène Delacroix, and

Honoré Daumier. In 1890, Edgar rented the topfloor apartment at 37 rue Victor Massé on the edge of Montmartre, an enclave of artist studios and galleries. Soon after, he acquired the two floors beneath him. This layout of his living quarters facilitated the mystery he created around his life as an intensely private man with a sharp-tongued social persona. His first floor was his sleeping quarters and strictly off-limits to all. He displayed his art collection and held salons on the middle of the three floors, which were impeccably furnished with cabinets of sculpture, cases of books, and walls covered with paintings. The top floor was Edgar's studio—messy and dusty, it was the private world of the artist and his models. In 1902, a young Pablo Picasso exhibited his work in a gallery in the next block. There is no record of friendship or intersection other than mutual friends and acquaintances. It is clear, though, that Degas's work influenced Picasso, who many years later honored Degas by putting his dapper figure amongst female nudes in brothel scene etchings.

Photography was commercially introduced in 1839. It had moved past the early cyanotypes to daguerreotypes, and by the time Degas was experimenting in the 1890s, the technology was much advanced and equipment more portable. Edgar had made many visits to the racetrack to sketch the horses. Now he studied the series photographs of horses in motion made by Eadweard Muybridge, an English photographer, for accuracy of movement. Degas purchased camera equipment and used this medium to record his own theatrical inventions. Where he might have observed and sketched in a corner at a dinner party formerly, he now orchestrated scenes lit with moody oil lamps or moonlight. He photographed Cassatt and himself. He posed his friends, rearranged furniture, and photographed them. It was as if he were creating paintings by ensemble.

In 1894, Alfred Dreyfus, a captain in the French military who was Jewish, was accused of spying and convicted for treason. Within a few years, evidence proved Captain Dreyfus's innocence, but anti-Semitism kept him from exoneration for ten years. The "Dreyfus Affair" sharply divided Parisians, and Degas's bias against Jews surfaced. His friends, especially the Halévy family, were appalled by his bigotry. Edgar lost much respect within the art and theater community. Degas became more isolated from his former friends and colleagues.

The following years were marked by the deterioration of his eyesight caused by retinal disease and the injury from the Franco-Prussian War years before. In 1912, the owners of his building decided to demolish it. Degas was forced to leave his three-story apartment and moved with his longtime loyal housekeeper, Zoé Closier, to one nearby on the Boulevard de Clichy. His vision had become so poor that he wore dark glasses constantly, unable to tolerate light. The move, though not far, was difficult for him. He expressed that parts of his life felt unfulfilled and that both time and opportunity were passing by. Degas created no art after 1912 because of his visual limitations.

> *"I have lost the thread of things...*
> *I piled up my plans in a cupboard*
> *for which I always had the key.*
> *And now I've lost the key."*

World War I was raging, with Great Britain and Germany fighting in France. Degas was unaware of the battles, as his vision loss turned him even more inward. Edgar Degas died in Paris at age eighty-three on September 27, 1917, and was buried in the Cimetière de Montmartre. He left a body of work that was innovative and masterful. France declared Edgar Degas a national treasure. Mary Cassatt wrote of her friend of nearly forty years, "We buried him on

Saturday, a beautiful sunshine, a little crowd of friends and admirers, all very quiet and peaceful in the midst of this dreadful upheaval of which he was barely conscious." Degas and Cassatt took the details of their long relationship to the grave. She burned all of their correspondence before she died.

Degas was an aloof man. This may have given him the advantage of acute observation. His work does not portray romanticized life. It takes the viewer backstage in the theater or to a seat in the balcony. The milliner's shop is not full of elegant displays of fashionable hats; the women are tucked in the darkness of the shop with the rich colors of ribbons and trim cascading off the worktable that dominates the foreground. The horses, bred for perfection and to race, are seen from behind, skittish in the moment before the gate opens. His portraits often give the sense that the subject is about to speak. Degas devoted his life to his art and left us a vibrant dialogue.

"Conversation in real life is full of half-finished sentences and overlapping talk. Why shouldn't painting be too?"